AF439550

Are There Enough Apples to Share?

Learn to Compare!

Math Book for Kindergarten

Children's Early Learning Books

Let's learn to compare numbers using equal, greater and less.

= Equal means they have same amount
> Greater means more
< Less means fewer

ACTIVITY 1

Which box has greater number?

For each kind of animal below, circle the box with more animals.

Which box has greater number?

For each kind of animal below, circle the box with more animals.

ACTIVITY 3

Which box has greater number?
For each kind of animal below, circle the box with more animals.

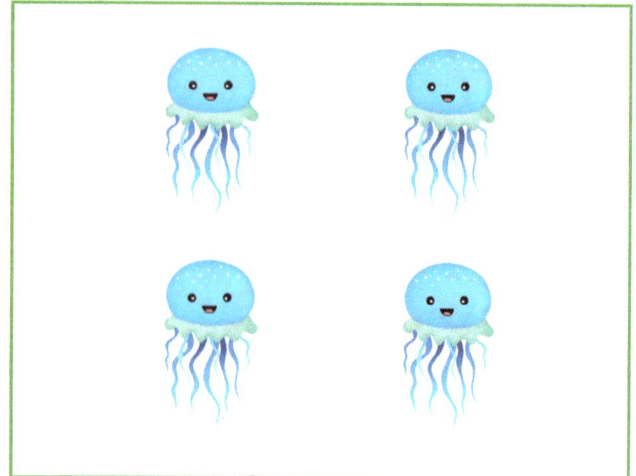 

Which box has greater number?

For each kind of animal below, circle the box with more animals.

Which box has greater number?

For each kind of animal below, circle the box with more animals.

Which box has greater number?

For each kind of animal below, circle the box with more animals.

Which box has greater number?

For each kind of animal below, circle the box with more animals.

Which box has greater number?

For each kind of animal below, circle the box with more animals.

ACTIVITY 9

Which box has greater number?

For each kind of animal below, circle the box with more animals.

Which box has greater number?

For each kind of animal below, circle the box with more animals.

ACTIVITY II

Which box has lesser number?
For each kind of fruit below, circle the box with less fruits.

ACTIVITY 12

Which box has **lesser** number?

For each kind of fruit below, circle the box with less fruits.

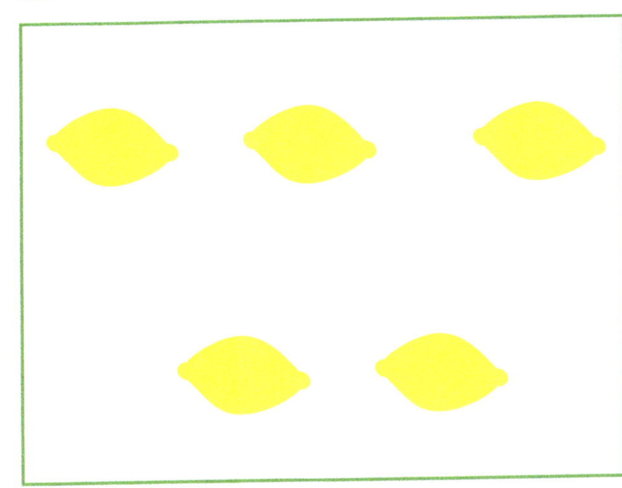

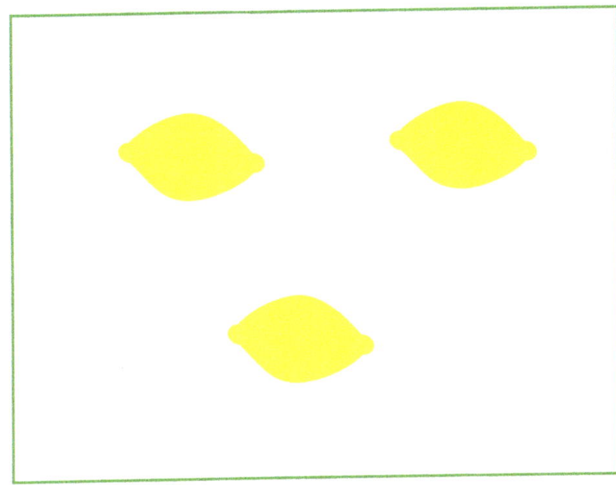

ACTIVITY 13

Which box has lesser number?

For each kind of fruit below, circle the box with less fruits.

Which box has lesser number?

For each kind of fruit below, circle the box with less fruits.

Which box has lesser number?

For each kind of fruit below, circle the box with less fruits.

ACTIVITY 16

Which box has **lesser** number?

For each kind of fruit below, circle the box with less fruits.

 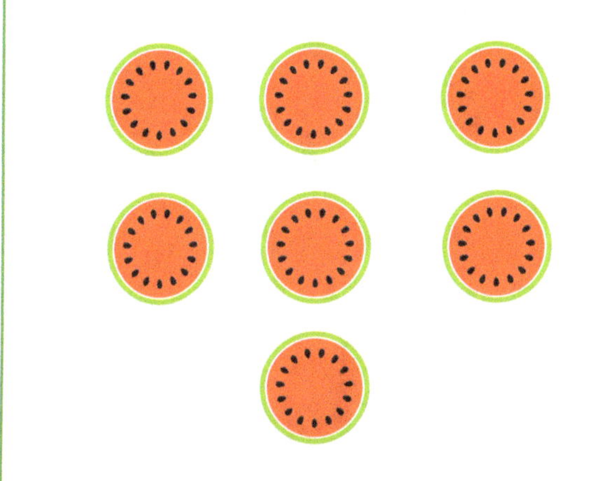

Which box has **lesser** number?

For each kind of fruit below, circle the box with less fruits.

Which box has **lesser** number?

For each kind of fruit below, circle the box with less fruits.

Which box has **lesser** number?

For each kind of fruit below, circle the box with less fruits.

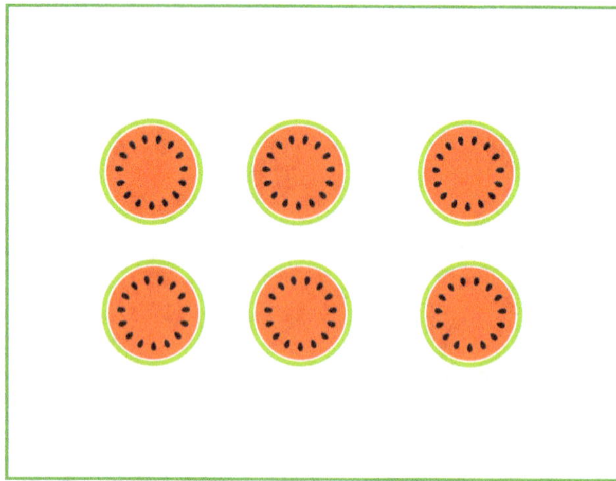

Which box has lesser number?

For each kind of fruit below, circle the box with less fruits.

ACTIVITY 21

Count the square in the box below.

Identify each group that contains less than, greater than or equal to the number of squares in the box. Circle your answer.

less than   more than   equal to | less than   more than   equal to

ACTIVITY 22

Count the circle in the box below.

Identify each group that contains less than, greater than or equal to the number of circles in the box. Circle your answer.

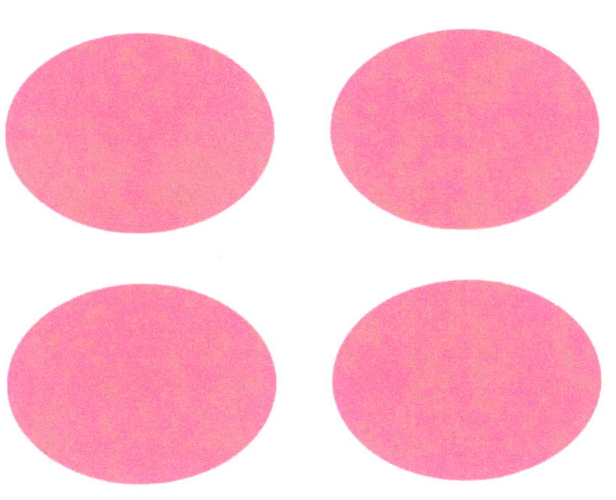

less than   more than   equal to | less than   more than   equal to

Count the triangle in the box below.

Identify each group that contains less than, greater than or equal to the number of triangles in the box. Circle your answer.

less than   more than   equal to | less than   more than   equal to

ACTIVITY 24

Count the heart in the box below.

Identify each group that contains less than, greater than or equal to the number of hearts in the box. Circle your answer.

less than   more than   equal to | less than   more than   equal to

Count the oval in the box below.

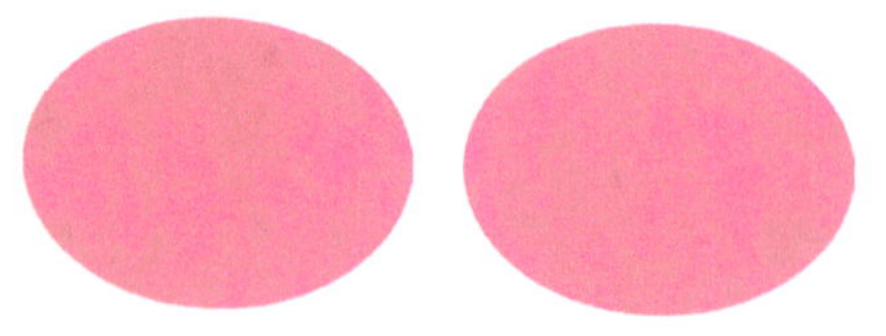

Identify each group that contains less than, greater than or equal to the number of ovals in the box. Circle your answer.

less than   more than   equal to | less than   more than   equal to

ACTIVITY 26

Count the **pentagon** in the box below.

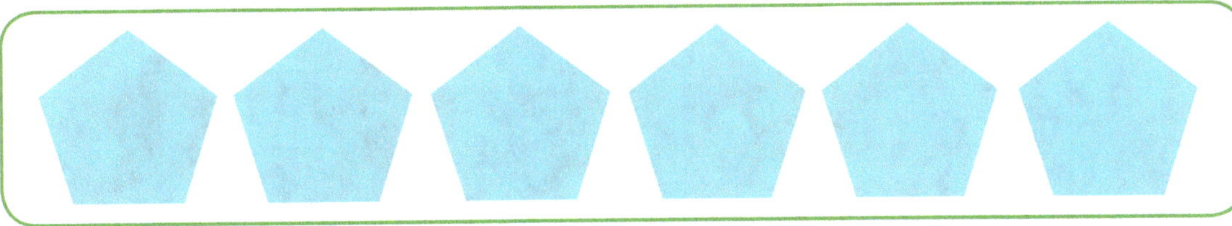

Identify each group that contains less than, greater than or equal to the number of pentagons in the box. Circle your answer.

| less than | more than | equal to | less than | more than | equal to |

ACTIVITY 27

Count the star in the box below.

Identify each group that contains less than, greater than or equal to the number of stars in the box. Circle your answer.

| less than | more than | equal to | less than | more than | equal to |

Count the hexagon in the box below.

Identify each group that contains less than, greater than or equal to the number of hexagons in the box. Circle your answer.

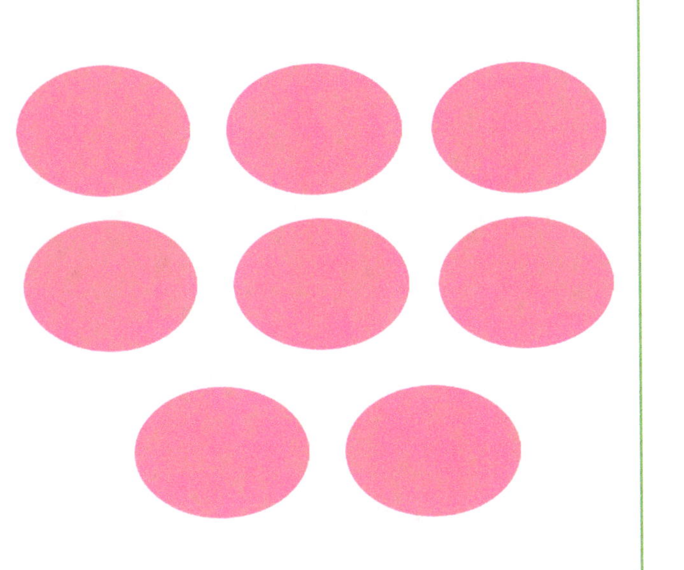

| less than | more than | equal to | less than | more than | equal to |

Count the **rhombus** in the box below.

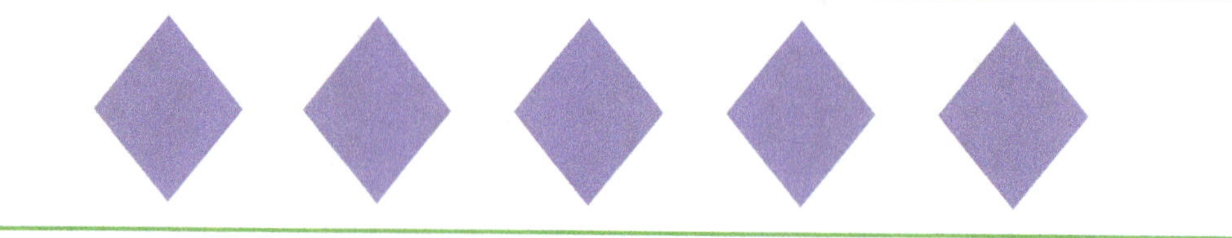

Identify each group that contains less than, greater than or equal to the number of stars in the box. Circle your answer.

less than	more than	equal to	less than	more than	equal to

Compare the fruit, then color the one having the **larger** number.

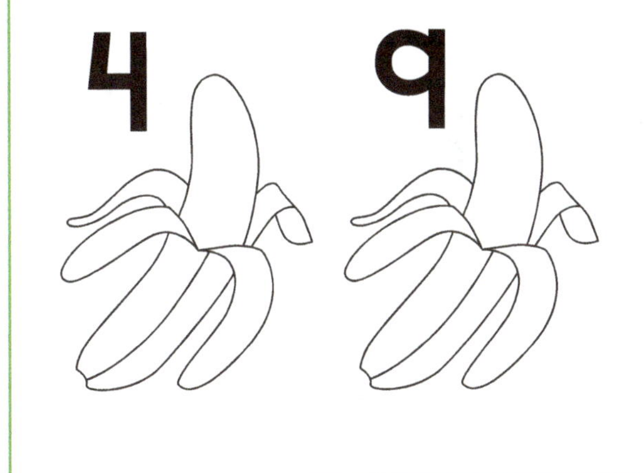

Compare the fruit, then color the one having the **larger** number.

Compare the fruit, then color the one having the **larger** number.

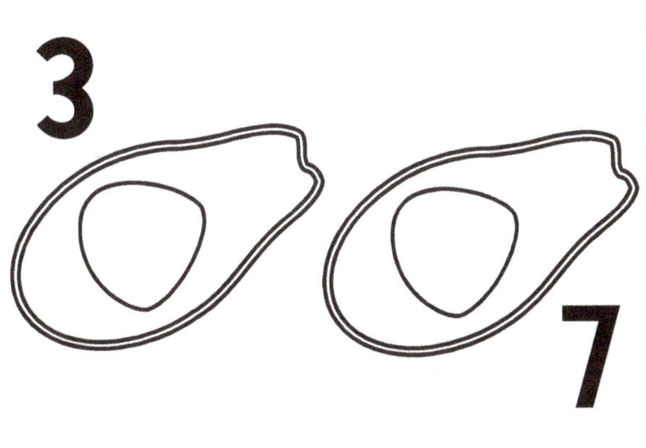

Compare the fruit, then color the one having the **larger** number.

Compare the fruit, then color the one having the **larger** number.

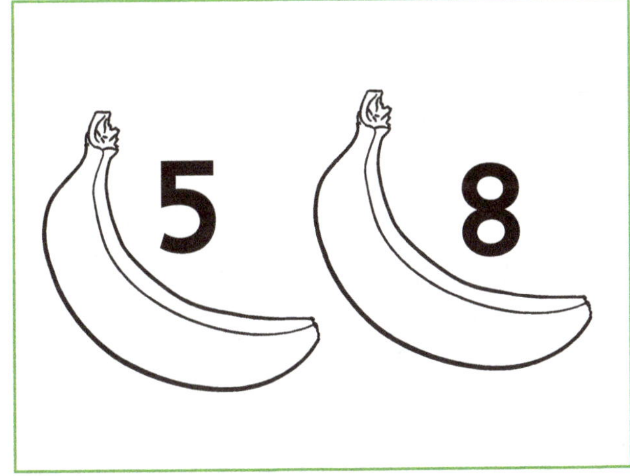

Compare the fruit, then color the one having the **larger** number.

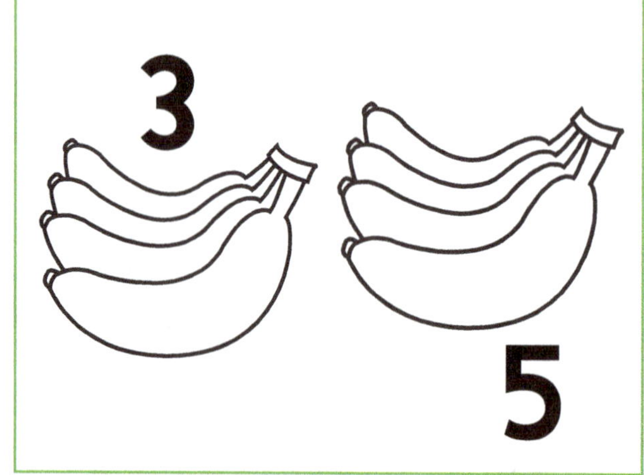

Compare the fruit, then color the one having the **larger** number.

ACTIVITY 37

Compare the fruit, then color the one having the **larger** number.

ACTIVITY 38

Count the **insects** in each jar.
Write the number in the box beside each jar.
Write < or > to show which jar has more insects.
< means less than
> means greater than

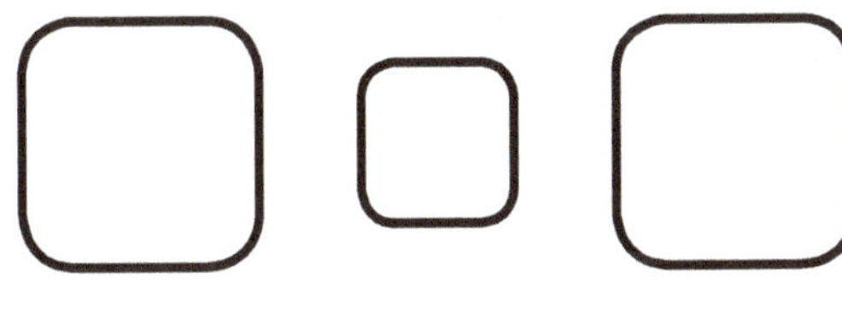

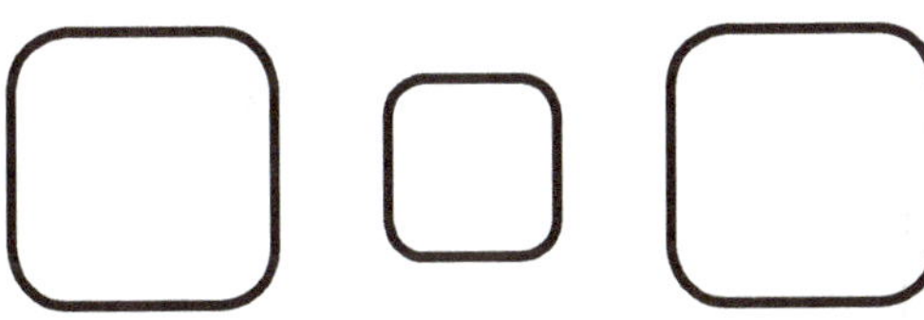

ACTIVITY 39

Count the **insects** in each jar.
Write the number in the box beside each jar.
Write < or > to show which jar has **more insects**.
< means **less than**
> means **greater than**

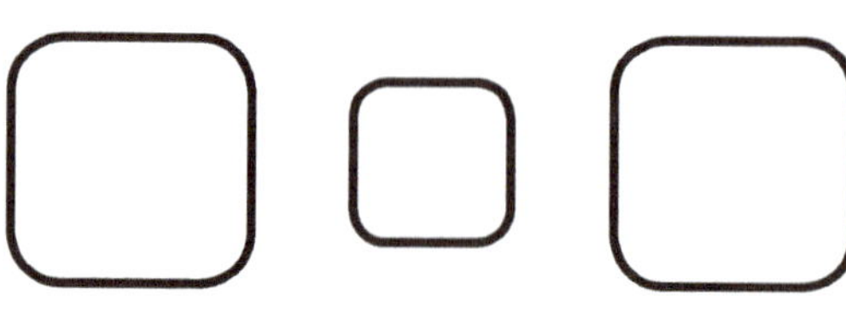

ACTIVITY 40

Count the **insects** in each jar.
Write the number in the box beside each jar.
Write < or > to show which jar has more insects.
< means less than
> means greater than

  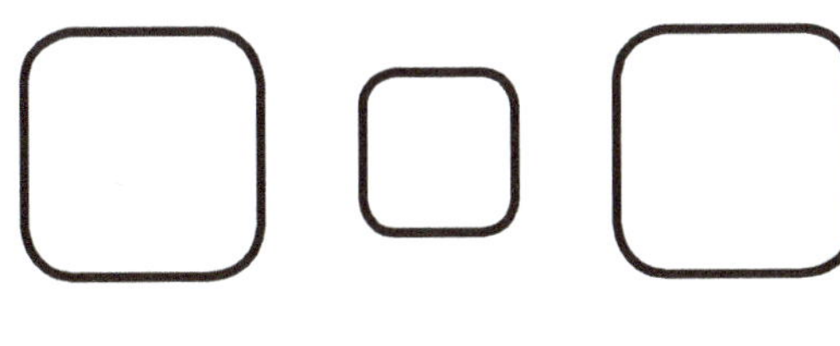

  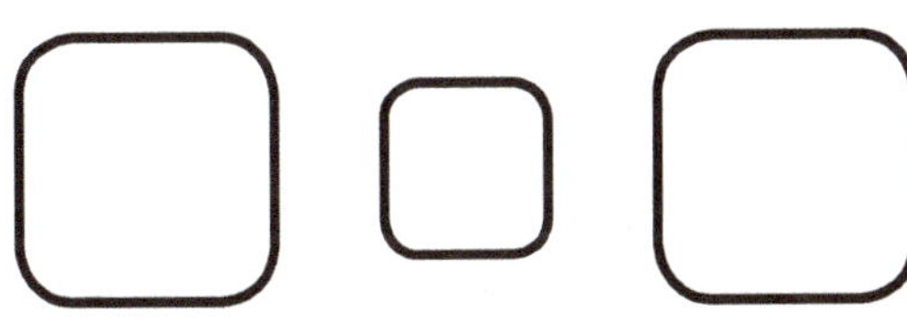

ACTIVITY 41

Count the **insects** in each jar.
Write the number in the box beside each jar.
Write < or > to show which jar has more insects.
< means less than
> means greater than

  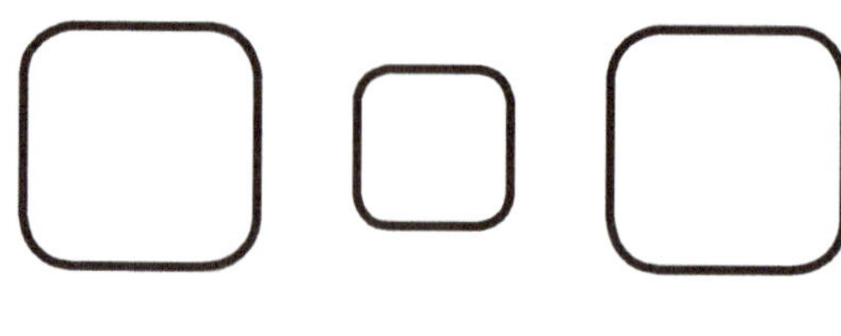

  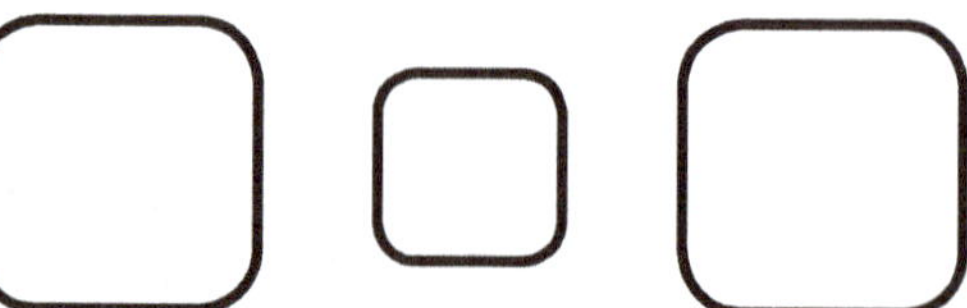

ACTIVITY 42

Count the **insects** in each jar.
Write the number in the box beside each jar.
Write < or > to show which jar has more insects.
< means less than
> means greater than

  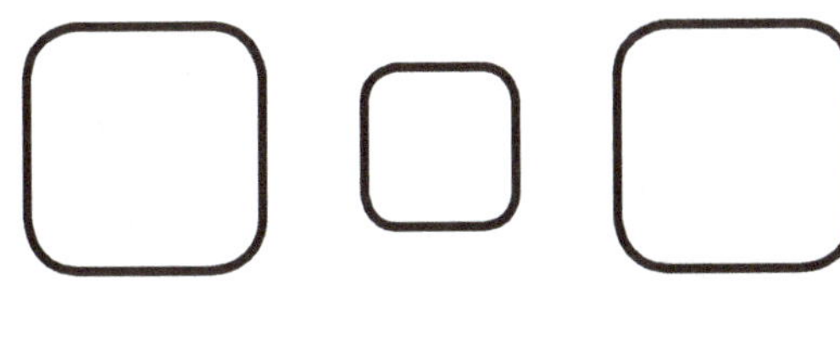

ACTIVITY 43

Count the **insects** in each jar.
Write the number in the box beside each jar.
Write < or > to show which jar has more insects.
< means **less than**
> means **greater than**

ACTIVITY 44

Count the **insects** in each jar.
Write the number in the box beside each jar.
Write < or > to show which jar has more insects.
< means less than
> means greater than

  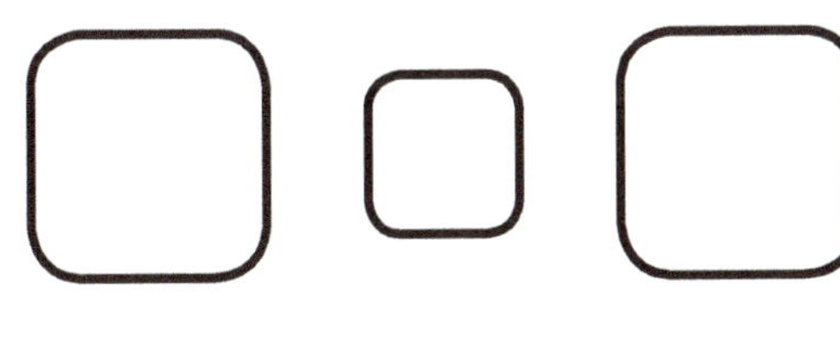

  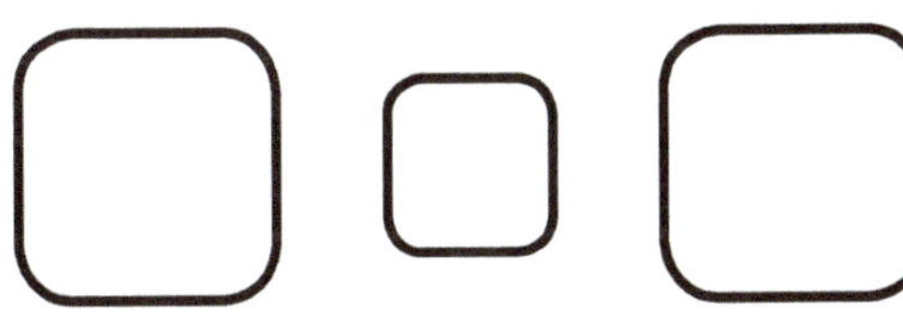

ACTIVITY 45

Count the **insects** in each jar.
Write the number in the box beside each jar.
Write < or > to show which jar has more insects.
< means less than
> means greater than

  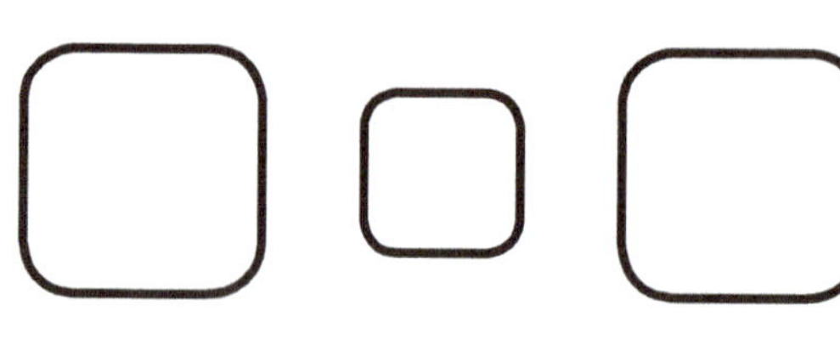

  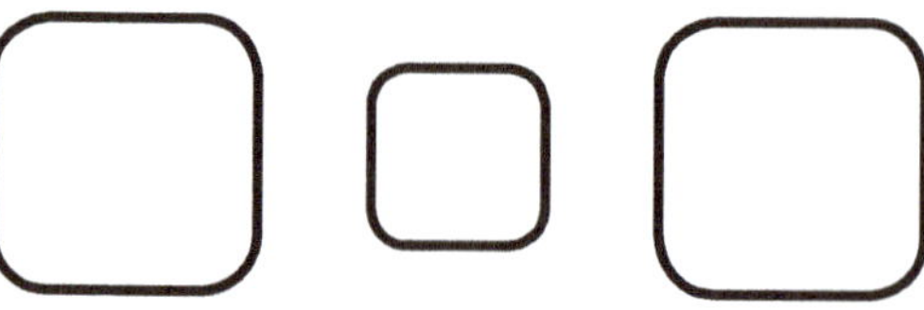

Answer Keys

Which box has greater number?

For each kind of animal below, circle the box with more animals.

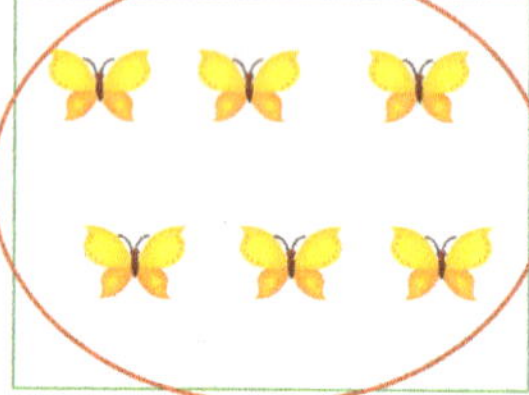

Which box has greater number?

For each kind of animal below, circle the box with more animals.

Which box has greater number?

For each kind of animal below, circle the box with more animals.

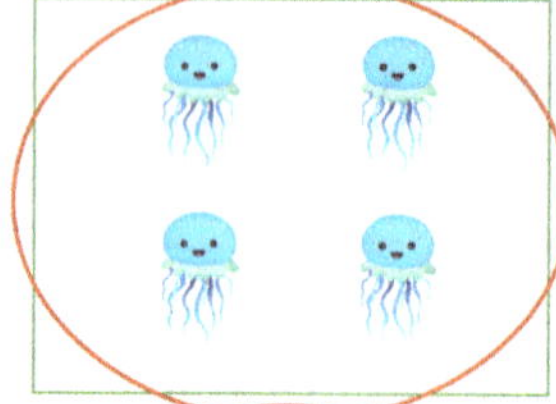
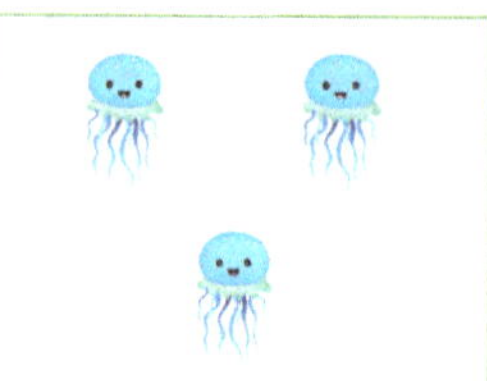

Which box has greater number?

For each kind of animal below, circle the box with more animals.

ACTIVITY 5

Which box has **greater** number?
For each kind of animal below, circle the box with more animals.

ACTIVITY 6

Which box has **greater** number?
For each kind of animal below, circle the box with more animals.

ACTIVITY 7

Which box has **greater** number?
For each kind of animal below, circle the box with more animals.

ACTIVITY 8

Which box has **greater** number?
For each kind of animal below, circle the box with more animals.

ACTIVITY 9

Which box has greater number?
For each kind of animal below, circle the box with more animals.

ACTIVITY 10

Which box has greater number?
For each kind of animal below, circle the box with more animals.

ACTIVITY 11

Which box has lesser number?
For each kind of fruit below, circle the box with less fruits.

ACTIVITY 12

Which box has lesser number?
For each kind of fruit below, circle the box with less fruits.

ACTIVITY 13

Which box has lesser number?
For each kind of fruit below, circle the box with less fruits.

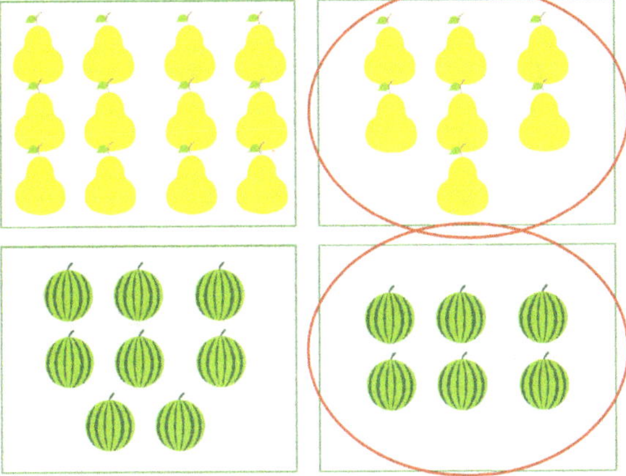

ACTIVITY 14

Which box has lesser number?
For each kind of fruit below, circle the box with less fruits.

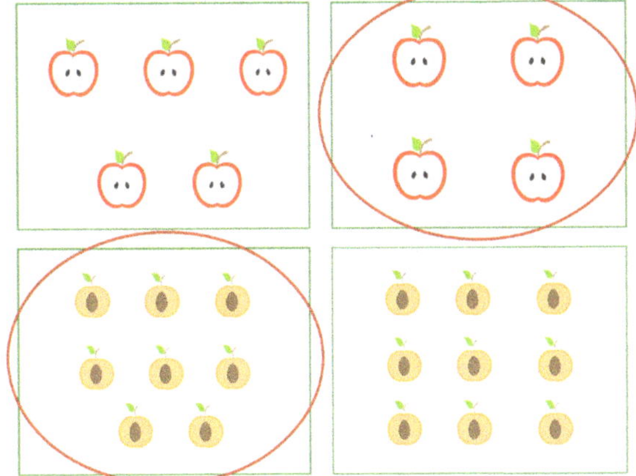

ACTIVITY 15

Which box has lesser number?
For each kind of fruit below, circle the box with less fruits.

ACTIVITY 16

Which box has lesser number?
For each kind of fruit below, circle the box with less fruits.

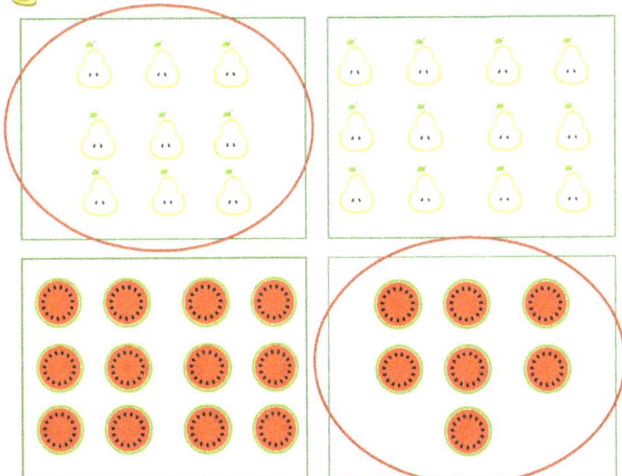

ACTIVITY 17

Which box has lesser number?
For each kind of fruit below, circle the box with less fruits.

ACTIVITY 18

Which box has lesser number?
For each kind of fruit below, circle the box with less fruits.

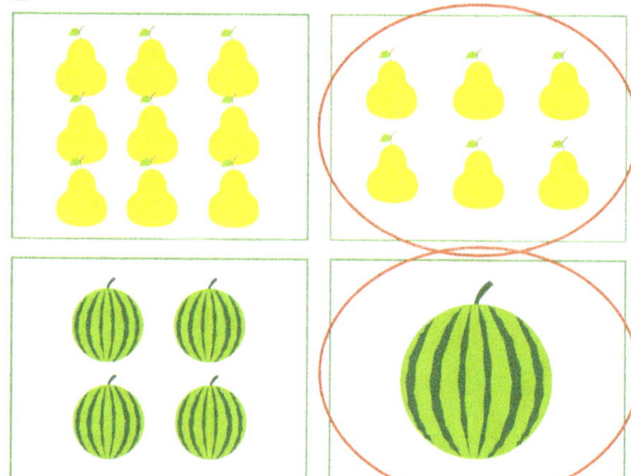

ACTIVITY 19

Which box has lesser number?
For each kind of fruit below, circle the box with less fruits.

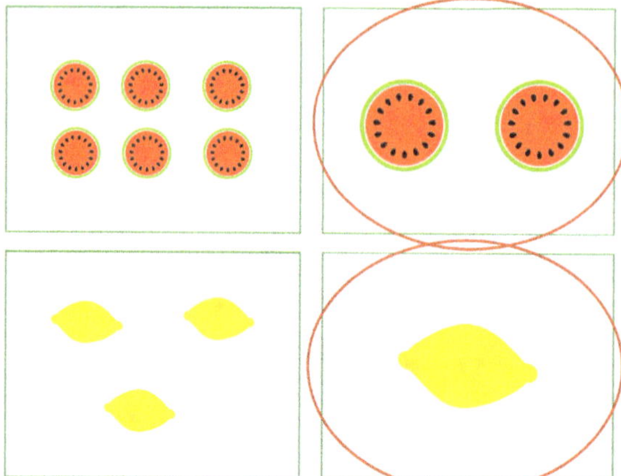

ACTIVITY 20

Which box has lesser number?
For each kind of fruit below, circle the box with less fruits.

ACTIVITY 21

Count the square in the box below.

Identify each group that contains less than, greater than or equal to the number of squares in the box. Circle your answer.

less than   (more than)   equal to | (less than)   more than   equal to

ACTIVITY 22

Count the circle in the box below.

Identify each group that contains less than, greater than or equal to the number of circles in the box. Circle your answer.

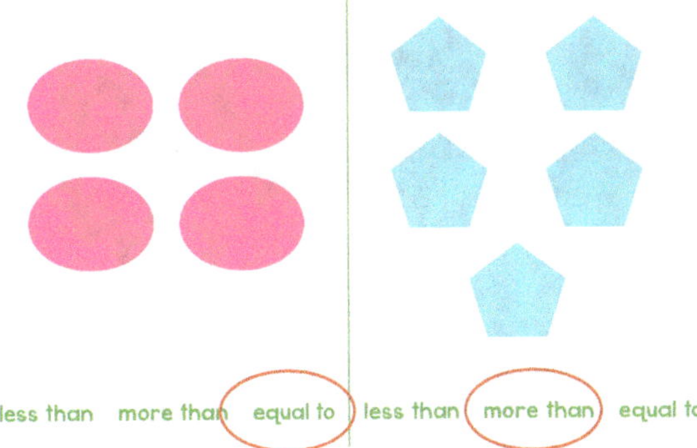

less than   more than   (equal to) | less than   (more than)   equal to

ACTIVITY 23

Count the triangle in the box below.

Identify each group that contains less than, greater than or equal to the number of triangles in the box. Circle your answer.

less than   (more than)   equal to | (less than)   more than   equal to

ACTIVITY 24

Count the heart in the box below.

Identify each group that contains less than, greater than or equal to the number of hearts in the box. Circle your answer.

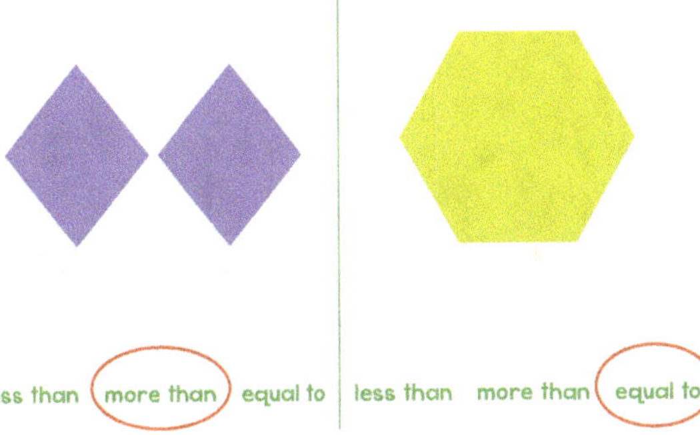

less than   (more than)   equal to | less than   more than   (equal to)

ACTIVITY 25

Count the oval in the box below.

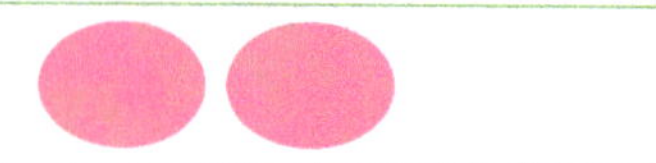

Identify each group that contains less than, greater than or equal to the number of ovals in the box. Circle your answer.

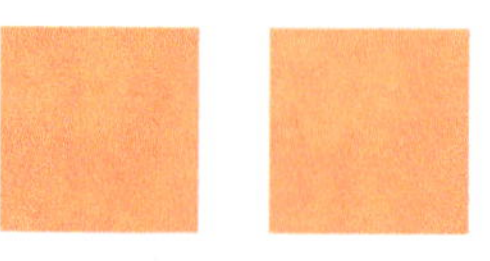

less than   (more than)   equal to | less than   more than   (equal to)

ACTIVITY 26

Count the pentagon in the box below.

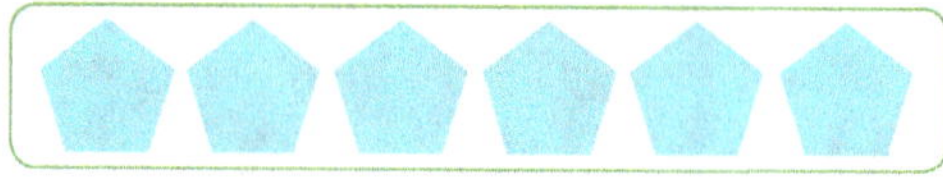

Identify each group that contains less than, greater than or equal to the number of pentagons in the box. Circle your answer.

(less than)   more than   equal to | less than   more than   (equal to)

ACTIVITY 27

Count the star in the box below.

Identify each group that contains less than, greater than or equal to the number of stars in the box. Circle your answer.

less than   more than   (equal to) | less than   (more than)   equal to

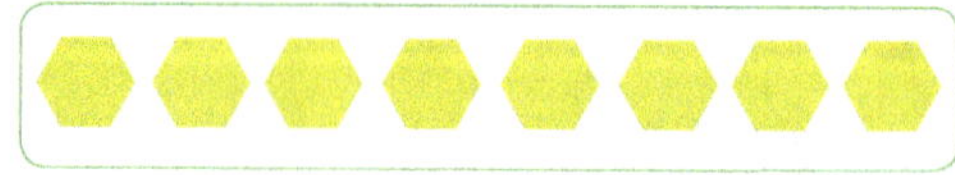

ACTIVITY 28

Count the hexagon in the box below.

Identify each group that contains less than, greater than or equal to the number of hexagons in the box. Circle your answer.

less than   more than   (equal to) | less than   (more than)   equal to

ACTIVITY 29

Count the rhombus in the box below.

Identify each group that contains less than, greater than or equal to the number of stars in the box. Circle your answer.

less than   (more than)   equal to   (less than)   more than   equal to

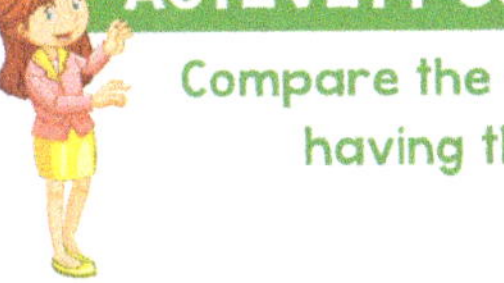
ACTIVITY 30

Compare the fruit, then color the one having the larger number.

ACTIVITY 31

Compare the fruit, then color the one having the larger number.

ACTIVITY 32

Compare the fruit, then color the one having the larger number.

Compare the fruit, then color the one having the **larger** number.

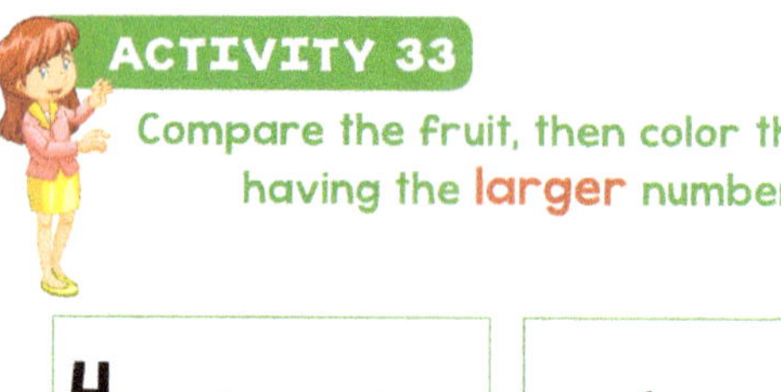

Compare the fruit, then color the one having the **larger** number.

Compare the fruit, then color the one having the **larger** number.

Compare the fruit, then color the one having the **larger** number.

Compare the fruit, then color the one having the **larger** number.

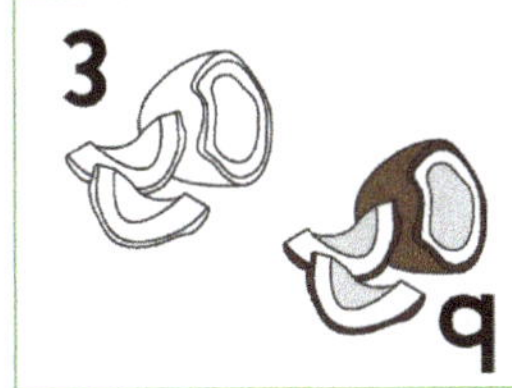

Count the **insects** in each jar.
Write the number in the box beside each jar.
Write < or > to show which jar has more insects.
< means less than
> means greater than

Count the **insects** in each jar.
Write the number in the box beside each jar.
Write < or > to show which jar has more insects.
< means less than
> means greater than

Count the **insects** in each jar.
Write the number in the box beside each jar.
Write < or > to show which jar has more insects.
< means less than
> means greater than

Count the **insects** in each jar.
Write the number in the box beside each jar.
Write < or > to show which jar has more insects.
< means less than
> means greater than

9 < 10

 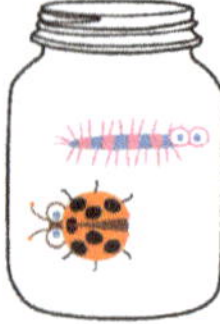  

5 > 2

Count the **insects** in each jar.
Write the number in the box beside each jar.
Write < or > to show which jar has more insects.
< means less than
> means greater than

6 > 4

5 > 4

Count the **insects** in each jar.
Write the number in the box beside each jar.
Write < or > to show which jar has more insects.
< means less than
> means greater than

4 > 3

2 > 1

Count the **insects** in each jar.
Write the number in the box beside each jar.
Write < or > to show which jar has more insects.
< means less than
> means greater than

10 > 6

6 > 4

Count the **insects** in each jar.
Write the number in the box beside each jar.
Write < or > to show which jar has more insects.
< means less than
> means greater than

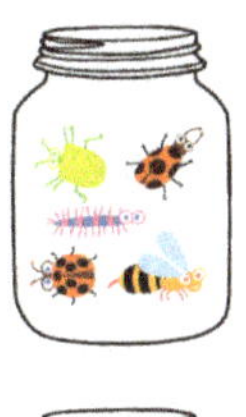    

5 > 3

4 < 6

Visit

BABY PROFESSOR
EDUCATION KIDS

www.BabyProfessorBooks.com
to download Free Baby Professor eBooks
and view our catalog of new and exciting
Children's Books